LILIES

BY
MARK SMITH
ILLUSTRATIONS BY JUAN LUIS G. VELA

A FRIEDMAN GROUP BOOK

Published by GALLERY BOOKS
An imprint of W.H. Smith Publishers, Inc.
112 Madison Avenue
New York, New York 10016

ISBN 0-8317-5557-1

A BOOK OF LILIES
was prepared and produced by
Michael Friedman Publishing Group, Inc.
15 West 26th Street
New York, NY 10010

Typeset by B.P.E. Graphics, Inc.
Color separations by Hong Kong Scanner Craft Company Ltd.
Printed and bound in Hong Kong by Leefung-Asco Printers Ltd.

CONTENTS

INTRODUCTION

The history of lilies, which goes back roughly 3,500 years, is primarily the history of a single lily—*Lilium candidum,* the Madonna Lily. Throughout the centuries, in societies as diverse as Victorian England and ancient Greece and Egypt, the *candidum* lily has been regarded as a model of ultimate beauty. Its pure white blooms have been depicted in every art form and have functioned as powerful symbols in both pagan and Christian cultures. To this day, *L. candidum* is widely considered the quintessential lily.

The exact native habitat of the *candidum* lily long remained in doubt, but it is now known to have come originally from Anatolia in western Asia. It was first cultivated for its bulbs, which were crushed and used as a medicinal ointment. It was in this form that the Greeks first imported the lily from Asia. Later they imported the bulbs themselves and began to cultivate the plant as a medicine and a cosmetic aid, then as a vegetable, and finally for the flower. Soon the flower became not only a favorite motif in Greek art but also the official flower of three Greek goddesses: Artemis, Aphrodite, and Hera.

From Greece the lily made its way to Europe by way of the Romans, who borrowed the lily, as they did many other elements of Greek culture, along with the Greeks' special regard for it.

It is possible that the *candidum* lily was also introduced to Europe in Spain, by way of Northern Africa. It would have been transported there from Egypt, where, as in Greece, it had been grown as a food and medicine. However, there is no question that the Romans were primarily responsible for spreading the lily throughout Europe, including England.

During the Middle Ages, through a hazy chain of associations related to the pagan reverence for the flower, the *candidum* lily began to take on symbolic meaning in Christianity. Whereas for the Greeks and Romans it had been a sign of earthly love, for the Christians it took on the meaning of purity and chastity and became the flower of the Virgin Mary—the Madonna Lily.

A new era for lilies arose in the eighteenth and nineteenth centuries with the discovery and introduction of several new species (wild) lilies from the Far East. The first of these to arrive in the West, in 1804, was *Lilium tigrinum,* from eastern Asia and Japan. Thereafter came *L. concolor* (1806), *L. longiflorum* (1819), *L. speciosum* (1830), *L. nepalense* (1855), *L. auratum* (1862), *L. hansonii* (1869), and many others, each of which added to the exciting new dimension of lily cultivation. Without doubt, the most important of these new lilies were *L. speciosum* and *L. auratum,* which offered more variety of color than the others and were somewhat easier to grow in the garden. However, despite sparking a new interest in lilies in mid-nineteenth-century England, *LL. speciosum* and *auratum* by themselves were not enough to establish the lily as a common garden member. Without strengthened hybrid varieties, lilies generally were still too difficult for the average gardener to grow.

Sustained interest in lilies as garden plants came only with E. H. Wilson's 1903 discovery of *L. regale,* a large trumpet lily from the Min Valley in western China. The Regal Lily, as it came to be known, was special because, unlike other species, it grew easily from seed. Thus lily growers were able to weed out the weaker plants quickly and create what could probably be called the first popular garden lily. Within a few years after its discovery, *L. regale* was being grown in household gardens across Europe and America.

Wilson's discovery not only made it possible for the average gardener to grow a lily but also provided fresh hope for the possibility of hybridizing lilies—a process that had eluded lily growers through the ages, giving lilies in general a reputation for being difficult, unpredictable flowers, suitable only for the expert gardener. By the 1920s and '30s a new atmosphere of enthusiasm and expectation pervaded the lily world. Lily breeders were provided new opportunities to exchange ideas on hybridizing, and more money than ever was being spent on lily research.

The most important breakthrough in the history of cultivated lilies took place in the late 1950s and early 1960s. Due to new methods of storing pollen and forcing late-flowering species to bloom earlier than normal, species lilies of nearly every kind were crossed successfully for the first time. The result is that over the past thirty years, hundreds of totally new hybrid lilies have been produced in colors, petal patterns, and flower shapes never seen before, and which are much stronger, hardier, and more easily grown than their species parents.

In these pages, you will find many species lilies and a few "lilies" that are members of the Liliaceae family but are not true lilies (members of the genus *Lilium*). You might also be surprised not to find a few so-called lilies, such as the calla lily; many of these "lilies" are not members of Liliaceae and therefore cannot be included. You will find quite a few examples from the group known as the Asiatic Hybrids. Most experts would agree that this relatively new group of hybrids is the most exciting thing happening in the lily world today. Generally speaking, the Asiatic Hybrids possess more fine qualities than any other kind of lily: they are the easiest type of lily to grow; they are very winter-hardy and disease-resistant; they yield more flowers per bulb than most other lilies; and they offer a huge variety of colors. Too, because of these attributes, Asiatic Hybrids are the most widely available lilies.

You will find the flowers arranged alphabetically according to common names. (Hybrid names are considered common names.) The hybrids also include a selection name, which indicates parentage, followed by the year of hybridization, when this information is known. The common names of species lilies will vary regionally and internationally, so always rely on the scientific name when ordering from a grower.

The enticing flowers pictured in this unique volume may inspire you to grow your own lilies. Use the "Lily Cultivation" guide in the appendix for reference, and your garden will soon be blooming with the special beauty of these outstanding flowers.

Aphrodite
Checkered lily

FRITILLARIA

F. meleagris 'Aphrodite'

~

Sometimes going by Snake's Head Fritillary, sometimes Guinea Hen Flower, *Fritillaria meleagris* is said to have one of the most beautiful flowers native to Britain. Like its relative *F. acmopetala, meleagris* has a thin, lissom stem and a few tendrillike leaves. In form its flower is very similar to the tulip, yet it is fully pendant. 'Aphrodite' is the pure white form of *meleagris* and is noted for being a strong grower. The *Fritillaria* genus is a member of the Liliaceae family.

APRICOT BEAUTY

LILIUM

(L. tigrinum x *L. x hollandicum)*
x ['Erect' x ('Maxwill' x *L. tigrinum*)], 1964

~

This fine cup-shaped hybrid is a vivid ripe-apricot color, with reddish purple streaks running the length of each petal. It is an unusual design among the Asiatic Hybrids, and perhaps most interesting when cut and mixed with solid-color flowers. 'Apricot Beauty' is excellent in the garden, too, blooming in June and July.

ARTEMIS
CHECKERED LILY

FRITILLARIA

F. meleagris 'Artemis'

~

'Artemis' is the pure pink variety of *F. meleagris*. Its large nodding bells hang on slender stems at heights from 1 to 2 feet, and its few leaves are long, graceful tendrils. The form is unusual and gives *meleagris* its singular, enchanting character. It grows in delicate, lacy clumps that stand out best in more open garden spaces. Perfect for the rock garden.

AVALON

LILIUM
'Hallmark' x 'Destiny,' 1978

~

Here is a lily of truly singular appearance. Imagine
the early morning sun on a field of freshly fallen
snow—the stark, disarming whiteness of it—and you
have something of 'Avalon.' It is star-shaped like many
other lilies, but its glowing white, set off so strikingly
by deep purple spots, makes this star seem to dance
with glee. It produces six to fifteen flowers on a
well-spaced umbel inflorescence and reaches 3½ feet
in height. 'Avalon' is disease-resistant, extremely
easy to grow, and remarkably long-lasting as a cut
flower. For an arrangement of rare elegance, try
mixing 'Avalon' with bunches of bachelor's buttons
or a few spikes of delphinium.

CHINOOK

LILIUM

[('Lemon Queen' x 'Mega') x 'Edith Cecilia'] x
'Enchantment,' 1972

The rich salmon color of this star-shaped beauty is
unusual in lilies. From the petal tips to where the
filaments converge, the flower goes from a waxy
translucency to a soft opacity, with a sprinkling of
dark spots toward the center. In 1973 'Chinook' was
judged the finest lily of the show at the Floriade in
Hamburg, West Germany. Despite its apparent
frailty, it has all the hardy advantages of the Asiatic
Hybrid; perhaps most notable is its ability to retain
its vivid but delicate color in even the hottest sun.
The plant can grow to 4 feet, with as many as thirty
5- to 6-inch blooms carried on the stem in a
candelabralike arrangement.

CONNECTICUT KING

LILIUM
'Connecticut Lass' x 'Keystone,' 1967

There seems to be a certain irony in the countenance of this flower: It proudly displays its beauty, yellow face fully open to the sky, yet the subtlest blush of orange appears on each petal, as if in awareness of some immodesty. 'Connecticut King' is an acknowledged favorite. It is a vigorous, easy grower with exceptional resistance to disease. Because of its purity of color and form, it is widely considered an outstanding parent for hybridizing. The abundant blooms crown a lush, leafy, 3-foot stalk beginning in late June.

EASTER LILY

LILIUM

L. longiflorum

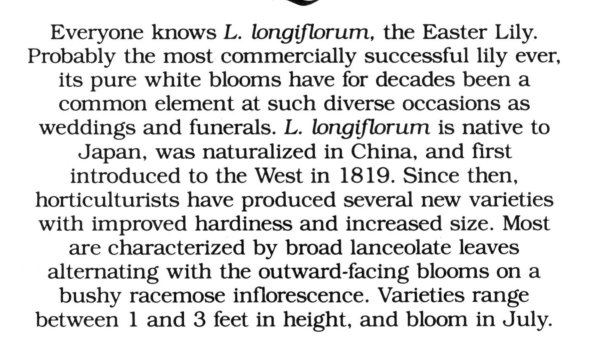

Everyone knows *L. longiflorum,* the Easter Lily. Probably the most commercially successful lily ever, its pure white blooms have for decades been a common element at such diverse occasions as weddings and funerals. *L. longiflorum* is native to Japan, was naturalized in China, and first introduced to the West in 1819. Since then, horticulturists have produced several new varieties with improved hardiness and increased size. Most are characterized by broad lanceolate leaves alternating with the outward-facing blooms on a bushy racemose inflorescence. Varieties range between 1 and 3 feet in height, and bloom in July.

ENCHANTMENT

LILIUM

'Umtig' x 'Alice Wilson,' 1947

~

'Enchantment' is the queen of the Asiatic Hybrids. Its bright nasturtium-red blooms with their oxblood freckles have made the plant the most commanding and popular hybrid lily, a ubiquitous delight in gardens across America and Europe. Another reason for its vast popularity is that it is very easy to grow. It thrives equally well in the garden or in a pot; it possesses exuberant staying power as a cut flower; and it is particularly disease-resistant. From ten to sixteen upward-facing blooms appear atop the 3-foot stem in June and July.

GOLD BAND LILY

LILIUM

L. auratum

❧

Essentially, *L. auratum* is a shiny white, flat-faced lily with a gold band overlay running the length of each petal's central vein; the petal edges are ruffled and slightly recurved; the white is lightly speckled with a red that matches the long anthers. As if this were not elaborate enough, many new variations on *auratum* have been introduced since the 1862 original. Some of these have crimson bands and have been dwarfed to only 12 inches on stocky stems, while others have very large bowl-shaped flowers and grow to 6 feet. Success with these sometimes temperamental lilies is not as easily forthcoming as with other lilies, but when blooms finally appear, in late summer and early autumn, you will find the effort has been worthwhile.

GOLD MEDAL

LILIUM

['Uncle Sam' x ('Mega' x 'Lemon Queen') x 'Edith Cecilia'] x 'Connecticut King,' 1971

~

'Gold Medal' is a rare prize indeed. Its nectary yellow petals have a subtle splash of orange that stands out in any garden. Look into the center and you'll see a refreshing lime green color fringed by a light sprinkling of dark, pigmented papillae dots. It is a star-shaped flower, with stiff arching petals. As a cut flower, 'Gold Medal' is a winner.

HONG KONG LILY

LILIUM

L. brownii

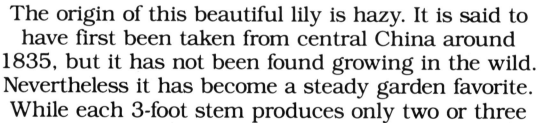

The origin of this beautiful lily is hazy. It is said to have first been taken from central China around 1835, but it has not been found growing in the wild. Nevertheless it has become a steady garden favorite. While each 3-foot stem produces only two or three flowers, these are striking, outsized trumpets of a pure white on the inside and an elegant plum color outside.

JAPAN LILY

LILIUM

L. japonicum

~

Sometimes *L. japonicum* is called the Bamboo Lily, not because it looks like bamboo but because in its native habitat—the alpine regions of Shikoku and Honshu in Japan—it grows alongside dwarf bamboo. Its bulbs prefer a soil thick with the fibrous roots of woody plants, which makes it an excellent lily to put beside border shrubs. The large funnel-form flowers are a lovely shell pink color and have a sweet scent. They are borne horizontally atop 5-foot stems in June.

MADONNA LILY

LILIUM

L. candidum

~

L. candidum, the Madonna Lily, has been ubiquitous as a symbol of sacred things throughout the history of Western civilization. It appears as a special emblem in the Talmud, and its bulbs have been found in the sarcophagi of ancient Egyptian mummies. In classical Greece it was the flower of Aphrodite, goddess of love, and of Hera, queen of heaven. The *candidum* lily took on new importance with the advent of Christianity, when it became the symbol of the Virgin Mary. Signifying chastity, it is found in much of the art of the early Christian period. To this day, the pure white trumpets of the Madonna Lily are widely used at sacred occasions such as weddings and funerals. For the garden it is an exceptional lily, sometimes reaching 5 feet in height.

MELON TIME

LILIUM

'Sunkissed' x 'Connecticut Lemonglow,' 1981

~

'Melon Time' is one of the newer Asiatic Hybrids, having been introduced in 1981. The upright bowl-shaped blooms are of a color somewhere between salmon, melon pink, and orange, with the faintest scattering of dark spots at the center. From eight to thirty fade-proof blooms crown the plant in June and July, and these are richly accentuated by its lush dark green foliage. To look upon 'Melon Time' is a refreshing experience.

MONT BLANC

LILIUM
'Yellow Blanc' x seedling, 1978

~

As the majority of her Asiatic Hybrid compatriots march forth with proud vibrant colors and conspicuous designs, 'Mont Blanc' does a quiet side-step and slips into the subtlest hues: the colors of milk and cream blend to make a purest white on her cup-shaped bloom. It is similar to the lovely 'Avalon,' but without the spots. Up to twelve flowers adorn the 4-foot plant in June.

NEPAL LILY

LILIUM
L. nepalense

~

L. nepalense is a beautiful and exotic lily, originating in Nepal, Burma, and northern India. Its large pendant blooms are stained at the center with an intense maroon, which sets off the bright lime yellow of the recurved petal tips. As few as five or eight flowers adorn the plant at maturity, but lack of quantity is more than compensated for by the amazing richness of color and design.

ORANGE POT STAR

LILIUM
unknown

~

This beautiful Asiatic Hybrid was originally bred in
the Netherlands, but its parentage is unknown. In
color, its arching flowers are a striking blend of
yellow and orange. It is an extremely vigorous plant,
growing to 4 feet on a strong dark green stem
with thick dark foliage.

ORANGE SPECIOSUM LILY

LILIUM

L. henryi

~

This exotic lily was originally discovered growing in
the dense forests of the Ichang Gorge, along China's
Yangtze River. Its pendant, sharply recurved flowers
are an almost luminous gold-pink color, with subtle
yellow streaks and blood red spots. It is an extremely
vigorous and hardy plant. Once established, it grows
on spindly stems as high as 8 feet and produces
dozens of beautiful blooms.

PARDANTHINA LILY

NOMOCHARIS

N. pardanthina

~

Exotic and temperamental in its growing habits, *Nomocharis pardanthina* originates on the high meadows of southeastern Tibet, western China, and northern Burma. It is closely related to the true lilies, yet in general appearance it is more like the *Odontoglossum* orchid. *Pardanthina*'s flower is a charming lavender-pink, with dark violet spots that intensify toward the center; its broad but pointed petals have deeply serrated edges that give a beautiful lacy effect. *Pardanthina* is difficult to grow, a breeze to enjoy.

PINK SHOWY LILY

LILIUM

L. speciosum rubrum

~

The rich pink flowers of this Oriental beauty are
displayed on the plant with unusual elegance.
Delicate jointed pedicels radiate crookedly from the
bony stem; flat lanceolate leaves, placed neatly at the
pedicel joints, almost seem contrived but work
perfectly to set off the ruffled chinalike blooms.

PRELUDE

LILIUM

'Joan Evans' x 'Connecticut King,' 1980

If you think this flower is beautiful when it first opens, just consider that its striking solid yellow intensifies with age. It starts out a cool lemony color and slowly climbs to its chromatic height—a rich deep yellow seldom seen in flowers. The wide-open, star-shaped blooms can be 6 inches in diameter and number as many as fifteen on a stalk.

RED MORNING STAR LILY

LILIUM

L. concolor

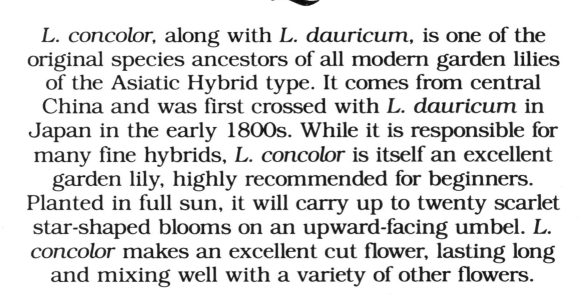

L. concolor, along with *L. dauricum*, is one of the original species ancestors of all modern garden lilies of the Asiatic Hybrid type. It comes from central China and was first crossed with *L. dauricum* in Japan in the early 1800s. While it is responsible for many fine hybrids, *L. concolor* is itself an excellent garden lily, highly recommended for beginners. Planted in full sun, it will carry up to twenty scarlet star-shaped blooms on an upward-facing umbel. *L. concolor* makes an excellent cut flower, lasting long and mixing well with a variety of other flowers.

REDWOOD LILY

LILIUM

L. rubescens

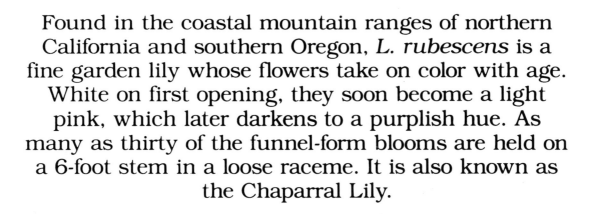

Found in the coastal mountain ranges of northern
California and southern Oregon, *L. rubescens* is a
fine garden lily whose flowers take on color with age.
White on first opening, they soon become a light
pink, which later darkens to a purplish hue. As
many as thirty of the funnel-form blooms are held on
a 6-foot stem in a loose raceme. It is also known as
the Chaparral Lily.

REGAL LILY

LILIUM

L. regale

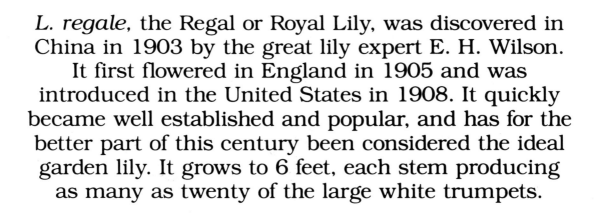

L. regale, the Regal or Royal Lily, was discovered in China in 1903 by the great lily expert E. H. Wilson. It first flowered in England in 1905 and was introduced in the United States in 1908. It quickly became well established and popular, and has for the better part of this century been considered the ideal garden lily. It grows to 6 feet, each stem producing as many as twenty of the large white trumpets.

ROSE BEAUTY

ERYTHRONIUM
E. revoltum 'Rose Beauty'

~

'Rose Beauty' is one of the finest examples of the popular Trout Lily, of which there are several forms and hybrids. It comes from the subalpine woodland regions of the northwestern United States, yet like many trout lilies its exact ancestry remains a subject of speculation. Its flowers are lovely pink stars, about 2 inches in diameter, with a semi-pendant placement on the 7-inch stem. The large ovate leaves stay close to the ground and are beautifully marbled with white. This plant is perfect in the rock garden, in a solitary position where all its fine detail can be most appreciated.

ROSY LILY

LILIUM
L. rubellum

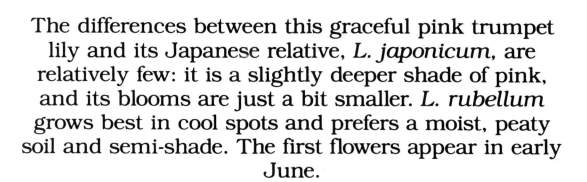

The differences between this graceful pink trumpet
lily and its Japanese relative, *L. japonicum,* are
relatively few: it is a slightly deeper shade of pink,
and its blooms are just a bit smaller. *L. rubellum*
grows best in cool spots and prefers a moist, peaty
soil and semi-shade. The first flowers appear in early
June.

SATURNUS
CHECKERED LILY

FRITILLARIA
F. meleagris 'Saturnus'

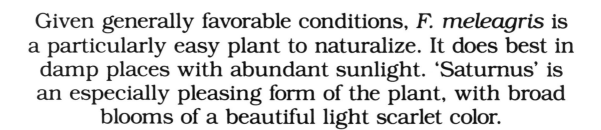

Given generally favorable conditions, *F. meleagris* is
a particularly easy plant to naturalize. It does best in
damp places with abundant sunlight. 'Saturnus' is
an especially pleasing form of the plant, with broad
blooms of a beautiful light scarlet color.

SNAKE'S HEAD FRITILLARY

FRITILLARIA

F. acmopetala

～

Acmopetala is easily the most unusual and frail-looking species of the *Fritillaria* genus. Its thin 1½-foot stems curve like charmed snakes and have a few long, tentaclelike leaves. The nodding flowers are bell-shaped and have slightly curved petal tips that give the plant an elfin look. Generally opalescent, the blooms are two-toned—the outer petals being jade green, the inner ones puce. *Acmopetala* is less a showy plant than one to be studied for its beauty.

SUNRAY

LILIUM

'Connecticut Lass' x 'Keystone,' 1965

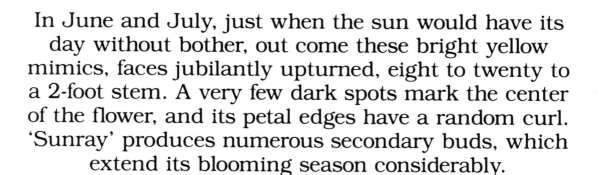

In June and July, just when the sun would have its day without bother, out come these bright yellow mimics, faces jubilantly upturned, eight to twenty to a 2-foot stem. A very few dark spots mark the center of the flower, and its petal edges have a random curl. 'Sunray' produces numerous secondary buds, which extend its blooming season considerably.

TALIEN LILY

LILIUM

L. taliense

This unusual Asian beauty gets its name from the
Tali mountain range in China's northeastern Yunnan
province. Its creamy white blooms are thickly
spotted with a beautiful deep purple and eventually
recurve so acutely as to produce six perfect ringlets.
The mature *L. taliense* can reach a height of 5 feet
and produce as many as twenty fragrant blossoms
on its pendulous racemose inflorescence.

TSINGTAO LILY

LILIUM

L. tsingtauense

~

An untrained eye could easily mistake this star-shaped species lily for one of the Asiatic Hybrids. It is a vivid orange upward-facing flower with wine spots—not unlike 'Enchantment.' Yet its thick waxy petals give it an exotic, unrefined character all its own. Too, the foliage is broader, more ruffled, and less uniform than in hybrid varieties. It comes from eastern China, where it was first discovered growing among dense grasses and thickets.

TURK'S-CAP LILY

LILIUM
L. martagon

~

The *martagon* lilies are unquestionably the most popular and important European garden lilies. In recent years, several supreme strains have been produced that come in many beautiful shades of red, including a very attractive burgundy and a red so dark it approaches black. The flowers are fully pendant, sharply reflexed, and are carried on a tall racemose inflorescence. It is an outstanding lily for beginners, as it is extremely easy to grow and multiplies rapidly.

LILY CULTIVATION

1. Obtain healthy bulbs and plant with pointed ends facing upward. In warm climates, plant in September or October before the first frost. In cold climates, plant in November.

2. To protect lilies, arrange them in groups of ten or more near trees or large shrubs. Soil should be moist yet well drained. Most lily bulbs need at least two-times their height in soil above them. The exception is *L. candidum,* which should be planted in late summer in less than an inch of soil.

3. While most hybrids thrive in full sun, the majority of species lilies prefer a partial shade environment. Hybrids also tolerate a wide variety of soil conditions. However, plant *LL. auratum, japonicum, rubellum,* and *speciosum* in an acid soil. By contrast, *LL. candidum, henryi, longiflorum,* and *martagon* appreciate an alkaline soil.

4. Cover planted bulbs with leaf mold, peat, and water. In late autumn, cover the soil with mulch to protect from temperature extremes. In early spring, fertilize with nitrogen when shoots emerge.

5. Do not overfertilize, as this rots the bulbs.

6. Lilies are generally disease- and insect-resistant, but if aphid infestation does occur, use a standard insecticide. When groups of lilies are planted several feet apart, chances of further infestation are minimized.

7. Remove old flowers as they wilt to ensure that new seed pods do not start to form and drain the plant of valuable energy. When cutting flowers, leave at least two-thirds of the foliage. Continue to water as long as the foliage is green.

8. In autumn, all old stems and foliage should be cleared away. If you wish to replant your lilies, do so in late September for cold climates, and later on for warmer zones. *L. candidum* can be replanted only in late summer.

9. In late autumn, mulch the soil again for the oncoming winter.

10. Remember that lilies do not lend themselves to formal arrangements; rather, they look better as accents on the fringes of woodlands, in wild gardens, or on the borders of a home garden, mixed with delphiniums and rhododendrons.

LILY GLOSSARY

ANTHER
The shoe-shaped part at the end of the stamen that contains the pollen.

ASIATIC HYBRID
The result of a cross between two Asian species lilies, principally *LL. tigrinum, cernuum, davidii, maximowiczii, x maculatum, x hollandicum, amabile, pumilum, concolor,* and *bulbiferum.*

FILAMENT
The stalk of the stamen, which supports the pollen-bearing anther.

GENUS (PLURAL GENERA)
A group of closely related species. Lilies belong to the genus *Lilium*, a division of the family Liliaceae.

HYBRID
The result of a cross between parents that differ in one or more traits, i.e. a cross between two different species, a hybrid and a species, or between two different hybrids.

INFLORESCENCE
The part of the plant stem that bears the flowers and buds.

LANCEOLATE
Pertaining to leaves that are wide at the base and sharply pointed at the top; lancelike.

LILIACEAE
A family of flowering plants encompassing 250 genera and 3,700 species. The most important genus it includes is *Lilium,* the "true lilies."

PEDICEL
The small stem that joins a single flower to the main stalk.

PENDANT
A flower that hangs with its face downturned.

RACEME
An inflorescence where flower stalks are spaced evenly, one on top of another, to the top of the plant stem.

REFLEXED
A type of flower whose petals curl back sharply.

SPECIES
Here the term is used to mean a specific kind of lily that grows in nature, as opposed to an artificially hybridized lily.

STAMEN
The male organ, consisting of the filament and the anther.

UMBEL
Inflorescence in which flowers appear in a cluster at the top of the stem, their pedicels radiating from a central point like the ribs of an umbrella.

LILY CLASSIFICATION

All the species and hybrid plants of "lilydom" are officially grouped into nine divisions. The wide array of hybrids reflects the gardener's quest for lilies that will bloom under a variety of growing conditions.

Division I: Asiatic hybrids. These prize-winning garden flowers require little care but yield spectacular results.

Division II: _L. martagon_ hybrids. These are available in lovely colors, but beware of their odor. Plant on garden borders.

Division III: _L. candidum_ hybrids. Although these flowers are extremely disease-resistant, they are not widely available.

Division IV: North American hybrids. An ever-growing division, principally derived from _LL. pardalinum_ and _humboldtii_.

Division V: _L. longiflorum_ hybrids. All are white with trumpet-shaped blooms. They are not significant as garden plants.

Division VI: Trumpet hybrids. Based on Chinese trumpet lilies, they make lovely corsages and are recommended as cut flowers.

Division VII: Oriental hybrids. Crosses of _LL. auratum, japonicum,_ and _speciosum_ comprise this category. They produce surprisingly large flat or bowl-shaped flowers on 6-foot-tall stalks.

Division VIII: All hybrids that are not members of previous categories are included here.

Division IX: _Lilium._ All are true species lilies.